What Makes You So Special?

By Jennifer Morehouse

ISBN-10: 0994761503
ISBN-13: 978-0994761507

DEDICATION

To my son, Tucker.
And all his friends.

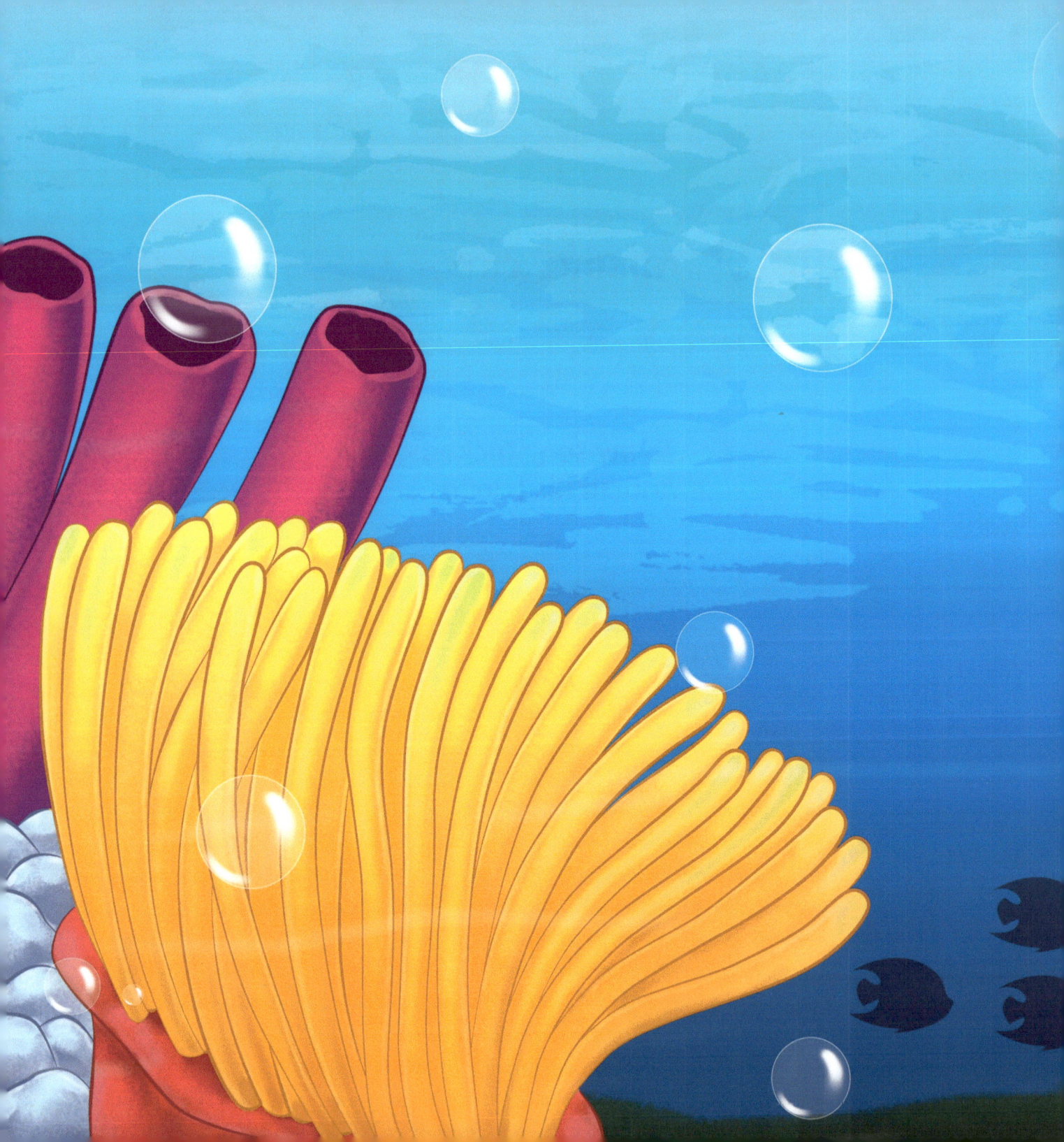

There are so many creatures in the big blue sea.
Not one as funny or goofy as me.
I'm a clownfish but I don't belong at the circus.
I live here in this plant, to me it's harmless.
That's what makes me so special.

I can live on land or in the sea.
No one keeps coral as clean as me.
I can be little or I can be large.
I have a lot of legs and two nice claws.
I may be a crab but I can make friends.
Jellyfish give me piggyback rides.
Everyone is different, it's easy to see.
Nobody is exactly like you or me.

There is so much to see on the ocean floor,
But clams don't travel or explore.
I sit in the same spot for a hundred years or more.
I have beautiful colors,
that make me different from others.
That's what makes me so special.

Oh, hello there! You scared me.
I'm not normally this big
but I wasn't sure if you were friendly.
I'm a balloonfish and I puff up to look bigger,
so I can make real friends a little bit quicker.

Way down deep is where you will find a squid.
For years people looked but rarely ever did.
Down here there's lots of room to just grow and grow.
Someday I'll be as big as a school bus
but I move very slow.

I'm not a starfish, I'm not a fish at all.
I am a sea star and I don't go far.
On rocks and coral is where you will find my family,
as happy as can be.

A seahorse is how people
know me. Not a horse on
land, I'm so small,
I can be really hard to see.
I don't swim that well
so I use my tail.
I hang on to plants
when the waves wail.
That's what makes me
so special.

We are jellyfish but we have no fins.
Our bodies are mostly water and we have no brains.
We don't go into the beaches on purpose.
When the waves push us in, we are helpless.

We have a long way to go, sea turtles never stop swimming.
For up to 80 years, we travel as long as we're living.
We have help from the currents to keep us flowing
and the friends we make along the way keep us going.

A lone octopus in shallow water is where you'll find me.
I change color and shoot ink
to make it hard for others to see.
What makes me special is that I taste through my legs,
but I don't mind because that's my kind.

We are butterfly fish. We're not sure why
because we don't fly.
We stay together to protect each other.
We have stripes on our front and on our back
so predators don't know where to attack.
That's what makes us so special.

As the smartest mammals in the sea,
dolphins stay together with family.
Some days we travel very far,
other days we play near shore and the sand bar.
No one else understands our language
but we still have a lot to say.
Everyone is different and we think that's okay.

We all come from
different parts of the
ocean and we all do
different things.
We all have special stuff
about us that makes
life interesting.

When we all come together,
what makes us different
isn't so easy to see.
We share this place we call
home and we want to keep it
nice for everybody.

WORD SEARCH

D	D	A	S	Q	U	I	D	Y	O
N	O	S	W	I	M	G	L	U	A
E	L	C	H	J	F	I	S	H	C
I	P	B	E	V	M	T	X	D	B
R	H	T	L	A	R	O	C	A	K
F	I	N	F	S	N	P	R	E	V
G	N	E	V	A	W	C	L	A	M

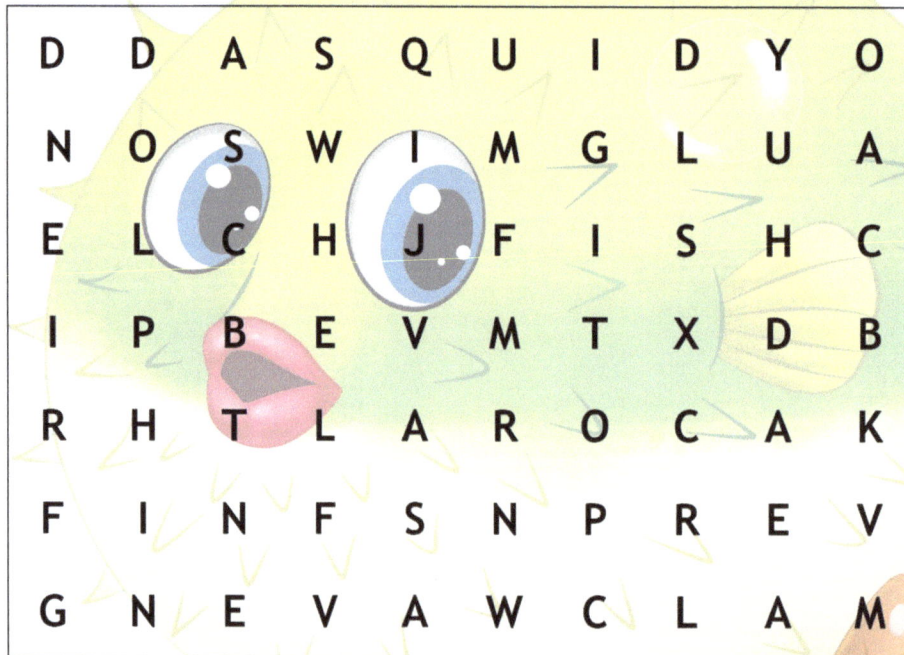

- crab
- wave
- family
- ocean
- fin
- clam
- friend
- dolphin
- coral
- squid
- swim

1. Sea stars can be found all around the world.
2. Balloonfish puff up when they are scared.
3. A very famous clownfish is named Nemo.
4. Crabs clean coral!
5. I wish I could shoot ink like an octopus.
6. Jellyfish have no brains.
7. Sea turtles always travel.

SECRET WORD

What is the SECRET word?
Put all the blue letters in the spaces below.

____ ____ ____ ____ ____ ____ ____

www.ingramcontent.com/pod-product-compliance
Lightning Source LLC
Chambersburg PA
CBHW042115040426
42448CB00003B/284